# TEACH YOURSELF TO PIANO SONGS

To access audio visit:
**www.halleonard.com/mylibrary**
Enter Code
7272-7537-5293-1283

ISBN 978-1-4950-3585-2

HAL•LEONARD®
CORPORATION

7777 W. BLUEMOUND RD. P.O. BOX 13819 MILWAUKEE, WI 53213

# ALL TOO WELL

This Taylor Swift ballad is quite spare in its construction. The four-measure introduction provides most of the material needed to play the song. Built on the chord progression G-D-Em-C, each hand stays within a limited range, as shown in the keyboard diagram below.

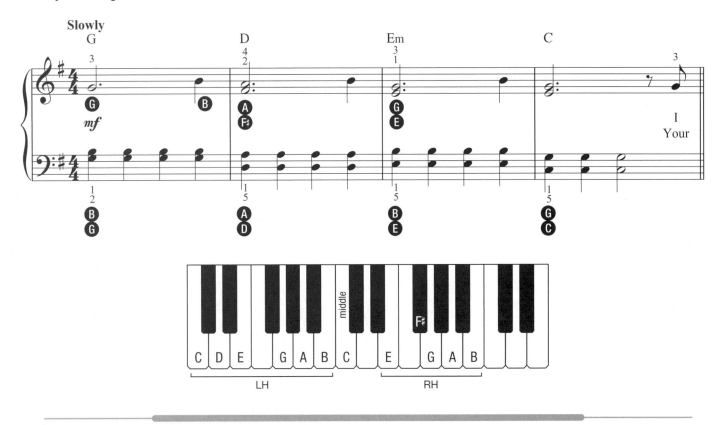

When the lyrics enter at measure 5, you'll notice the right hand stays in this beginning position, making it easier to concentrate on the rhythms that drive the lyrics. Observe the ties with care, to express the slow and subtle syncopation. Sing along and let your voice lead you.

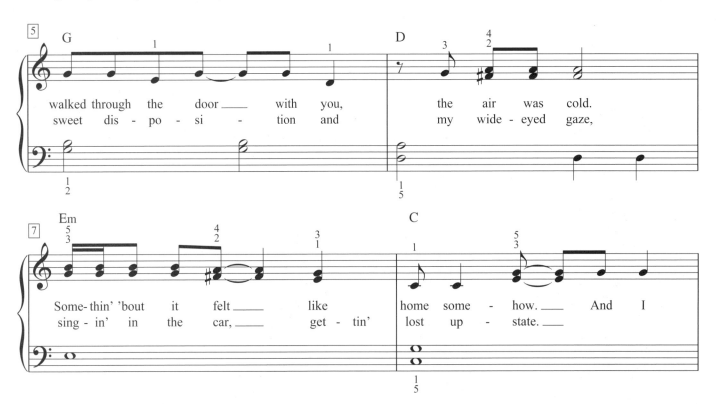

The next four measures are similar to the ones you just learned. Practice through the first and second endings, leading to the pick-up to measure 14, and the lyrics, "And I know…" Note that right-hand thumb moves to G to allow you to player higher on the keyboard.

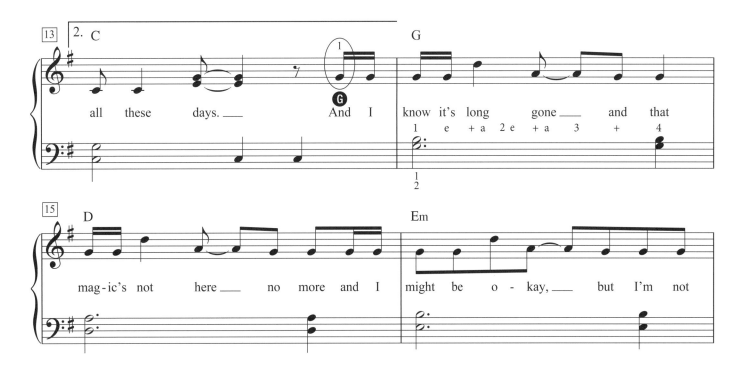

There's more syncopation in the melody here, and through the rest of the song. Remember, syncopation is an emphasis on a part of the beat that is usually not emphasized. For example, measure 14 has an emphasis on the "and" of beats 1 and 2. In slower tempos the syncopation is gentler, but still gives energy and forward movement to the lyrics. We've added some counting in measure 14 as a guide, but feel free to add in more counting, and listen to the audio to feel comfortable with the syncopation.

Although there's a small shift in position for the right hand, the left hand stays solidly in place to the very end.

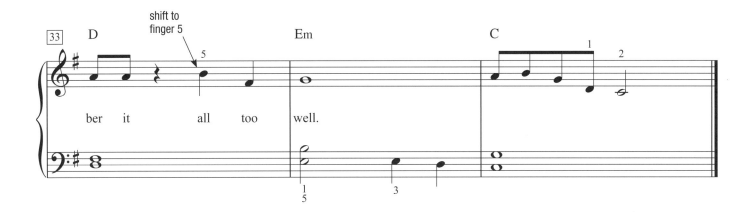

# ALL TOO WELL

Words and Music by TAYLOR SWIFT
and LIZ ROSE

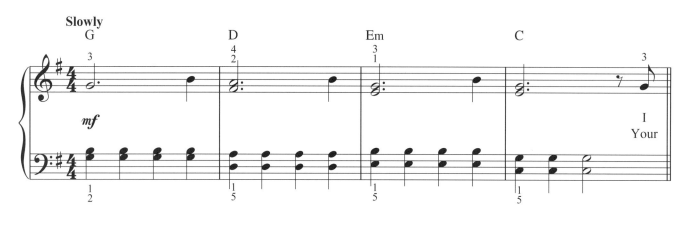

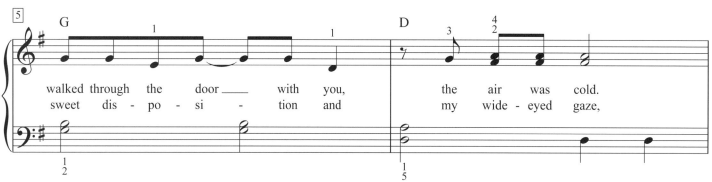

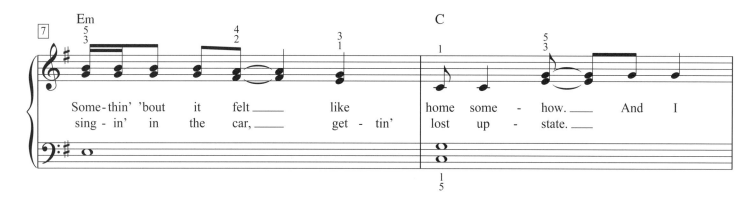

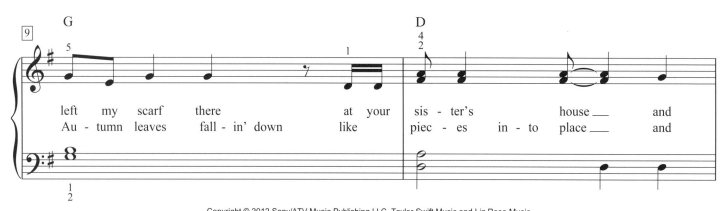

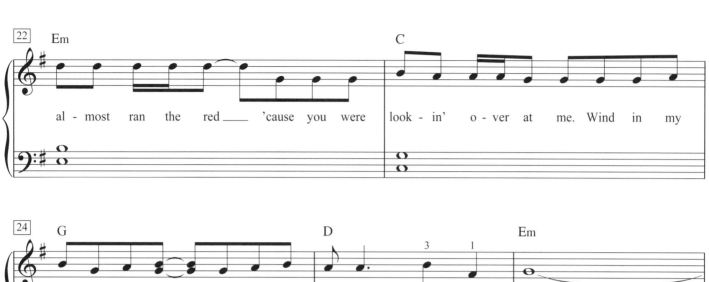

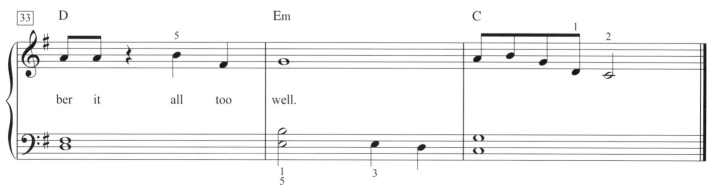

# DON'T KNOW WHY

Written by Jesse Harris, Norah Jones made this bluesy tune famous. Much of its signature sound comes from the use of **accidentals**—sharps and flats not in the key signature. Just a reminder, accidentals last for the entire measure.

Let's jump ahead to measure 5 where the lyrics start. Once you've mastered measures 5-8, you'll have most of the song under your fingers.

The left hand plays an easy chord progression over four measures. The chords change twice each measure. Right away you'll see the accidentals, B♭ in measure 5, G♯ in measure 6, and F♯ in measure 7. The natural sign in measure 8 cancels the previous F♯.

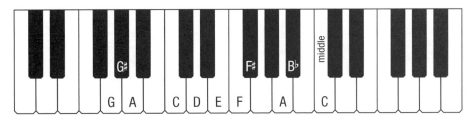

Spend some time playing these left-hand measures. Once you're comfortable with them (maybe even memorize them), take a look through the rest of the song. This left-hand progression appears in exactly the same way, seven more times, including the introduction.

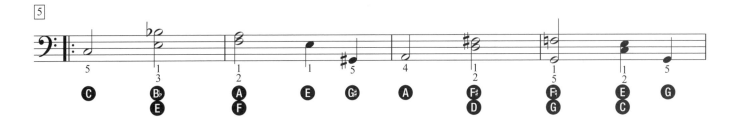

Now add the right-hand melody, playing along with the audio if you're unfamiliar with it, or just need a review.

Both the bass line and the melody changes with the pick-up to measure 17, beginning with the words, "My heart is drenched…" The right hand plays some beautiful chords against a single-note bass line. Spend some time getting comfortable with the chords, both with reading the notes and finding them on the keyboard. Play slowly at first, getting a feel for playing all three notes together.

You're on your own for the rest of this arrangement, but no worries! You've already learned the remainder of the song, and after a quick visit back to the introduction, you'll be ready to play from beginning to end.

# DON'T KNOW WHY

Words and Music by
JESSE HARRIS

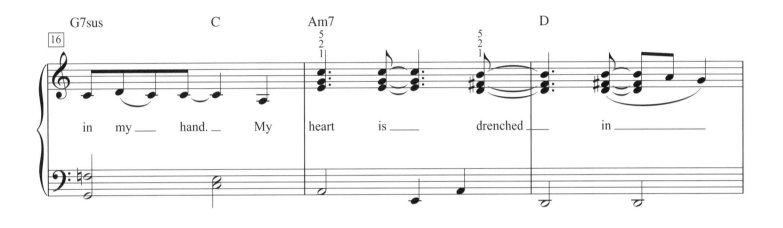

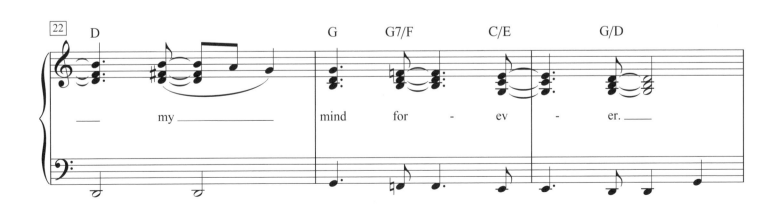

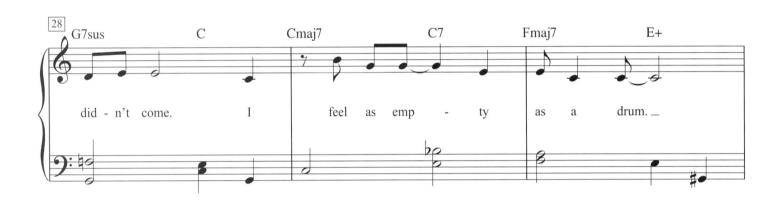

# IF I AIN'T GOT YOU

The sparkly right-hand triplets that open this Alicia Keys classic sound difficult, but they're easy to play. Once you've identified the first three notes of each two-measure segment, you're good to go. To find your starting note, place your right-hand finger 5 on the E an octave above middle C.

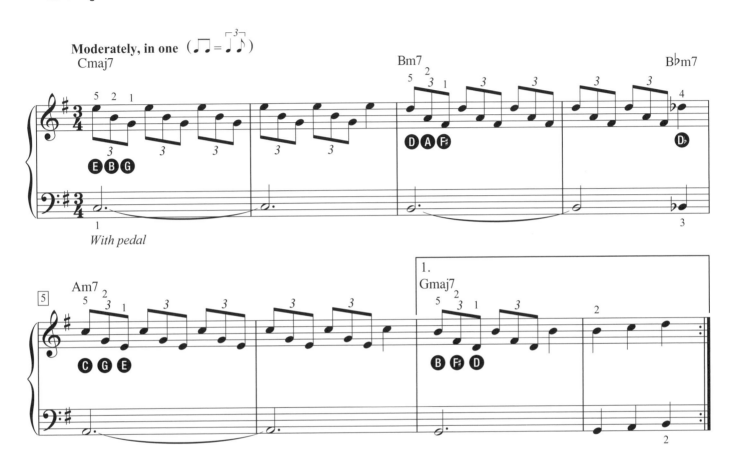

What makes these triplets so easy to play is the fact that every two measures the notes shift just one note lower. So, for example, in measure 1 you were playing E-B-G. In measure 3 you shift down to play D-A-F#. In measure 5, shift down to C-G-E. Keep your hand in the same shape as you shift, and play slowly until you can navigate the changes easily. Change the pedal each time the chord changes.

When the lyrics enter, the melody is notably low, indicated by the use of ledger lines whenever the notes are lower than middle C. This imitates Alicia Keys' distinctive vocal range. Always use middle C as a guide when reading the lower notes, and refer to our example here.

In measures 23-25 the notes move so low that it's easier to read them in bass clef, as they are all played below middle C. Watch for the bass clef in the right hand part at measure 23, and note that the treble clef returns at measure 26.

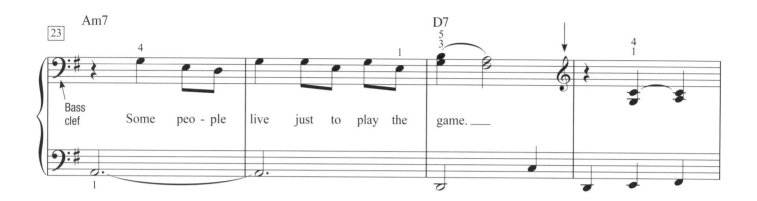

Beginning at measure 27, the left hand moves in 7ths. This beautiful harmonic motion is also easy to play. Find your first 7th, and then each measure, move both notes up or down, as written. The chord symbols above the staff are also a help with this. Remember the F♯ in the key signature. Learn the left hand by itself before playing hands together.

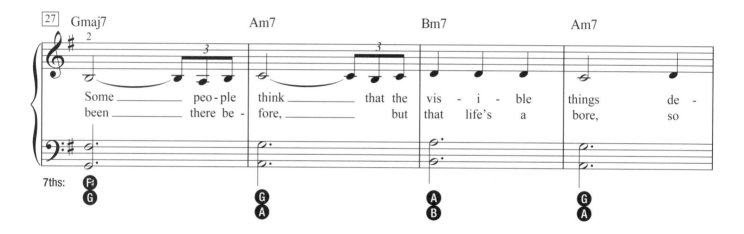

The right hand stays pretty much in one place for the last section of the piece, with a combination of single bass notes and 7ths. Try trading off with the audio as you learn this section, playing right hand with left-hand audio, and then the opposite. Sing along with the melody to help keep the groove moving, and enjoy the return of the triplets in the final measures to bring it all home.

# IF I AIN'T GOT YOU

Words and Music by
ALICIA KEYS

# ANGEL

This gentle song places the right hand close to, and lower than, middle C. Follow our hints below and you will learn the ledger line notes easily. Notice that the right hand follows a pattern. The top note, middle C, repeats while the thumb alternates between E and F.

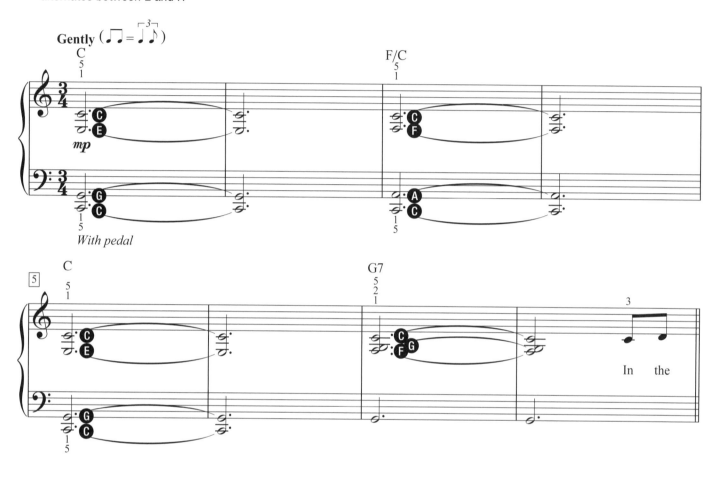

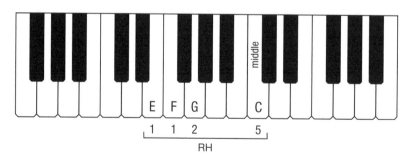

Your left hand mirrors the pattern of the right hand. The left-hand thumb alternates between G and A while the low C is repeated. Remember, you can use the opposite hand's audio track when practicing one hand alone.

Now play hands together, changing the pedal each time the chord changes.

When the lyrics begin, you will shift the position of your right hand. Be ready to stretch the hand, following the fingering given. Notice the small bracket in the right hand on the lyric "of." The thumb plays both F and G at the same time and then extends down to E in the next measure. Practice until this is comfortable.

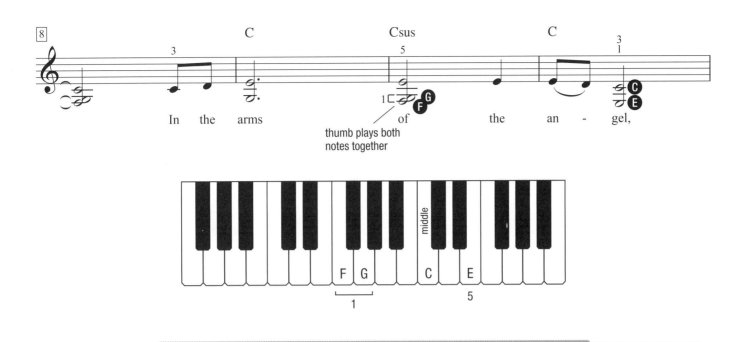

The next section also has a few right hand position changes. Follow the fingering to set your hand up for what comes next. The left hand is very simple and stays in one place. You might want to practice right hand alone before playing hands together.

Beginning in measure 17, the right hand plays chords for a full sound. Work on the jump that occurs on the lyric "endlessness." Notice that C and E are played with fingers 3 and 1 at the beginning of that measure. Then the hand shifts to play the same C and E with fingers 5 and 3 so the thumb can reach G.

Continue practicing in sections. Refer back to the keyboard diagrams if needed. There are two tricky places near the end (measures 37-39 and 41-43) with ties on the lyrics, "find" and "here." In both cases, the top note of the right hand is held (tied), while the bottom notes change.

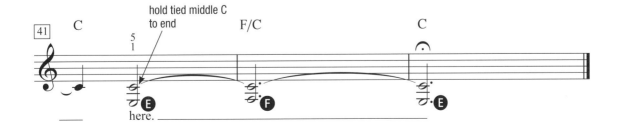

# ANGEL

Words and Music by
SARAH McLACHLAN

# BEAUTIFUL

Begin learning this lovely piece by working on the eight-measure introduction. Each measure contains a **broken** chord. That is, two of the notes of the three-note chord are played together, followed by the third note of the chord.

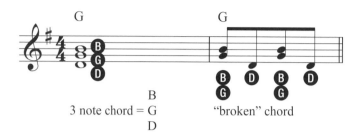

3 note chord = G
B
G
D

"broken" chord

There are three different chords in the right-hand part, and they remain important throughout the rest of the song. The chords are:

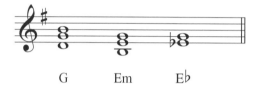

G    Em    E♭

The left hand plays whole notes moving down by step. Study the keyboard diagram first, and then play the introduction.

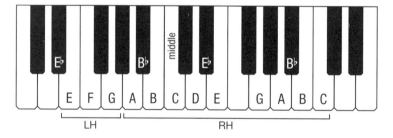

In measures 9-16, the right hand plays the melody. The only position shift occurs when G is played first by finger 4 and then by finger 2. In measures 12 and 16, you will need to extend the thumb to play E-flat. Slide the hand forward to reach the black key.

Notice that in measure 9-16 the left hand plays the same chord progression as the introduction. The left-hand notes are labeled in measures 9-12 below.

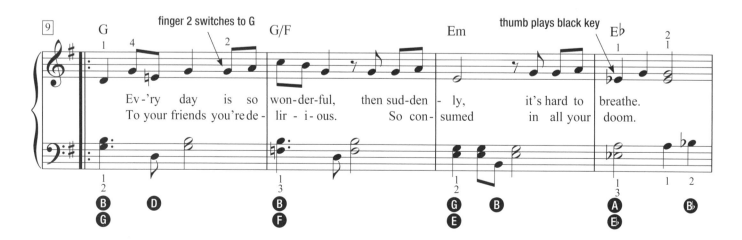

Ev-'ry day is so wonder-ful, then sud-den - ly, it's hard to breathe.
To your friends you're de - lir - i - ous. So con- sumed in all your doom.

There's only one more section of new material to learn. Measures 17-20 include a slightly different chord progression. C and Am appear before the familiar G-G/F-Em. The right-hand syncopation on the word "beautiful" is probably familiar to you, but if not, review it on the audio.

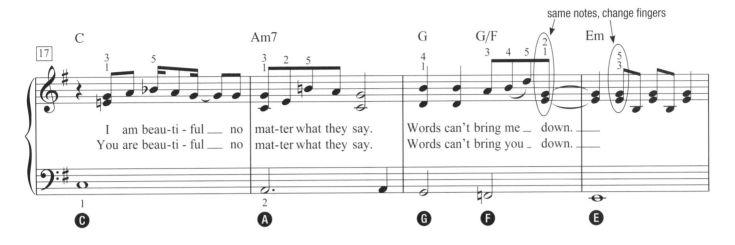

Measures 21-25 are almost the same as the previous four measures, and measure 26 to the end brings you back to the familiar chord progression from the introduction. Take your time as you learn this Christina Aguilera Grammy Award winner.

# BEAUTIFUL

Words and Music by
LINDA PERRY

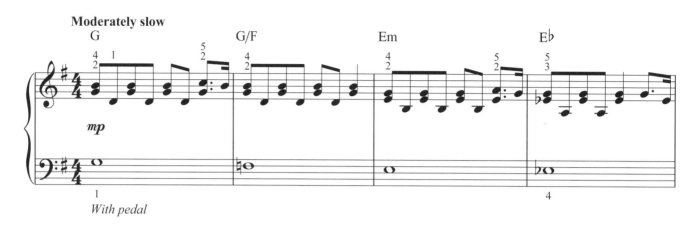

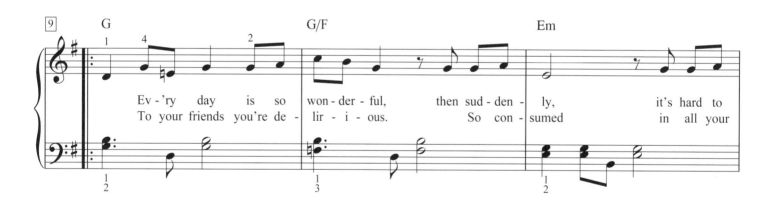

Ev-'ry day is so won-der-ful, then sud-den-ly, it's hard to
To your friends you're de-lir-i-ous. So con-sumed in all your

breathe.
doom.
Now and then I get in-se-cure from all the
Try-ing hard to fill the emp-ti-ness. The piec-es

# LOVE SONG

Sara Bareilles has been quoted as saying her biggest single "wrote itself," and with a little practice, "Love Song" will just about play itself too. Here we've presented the main thematic material: verse and chorus.

A strong beat and alternating hands make this song great fun to play. First, note that the eighth notes are to be played in swing rhythm, as designated at the beginning of the song. Your left hand plays octaves in the low register of the piano, and the right hand alternates those octaves with chords. A four-measure pattern repeats throughout.

Take a look at the left-hand octaves first. Starting on low G, an octave below middle C plus the G lower than that, you move up one note at a time over the first three measures, jumping down to low F♯s in measure four.

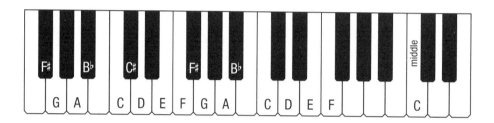

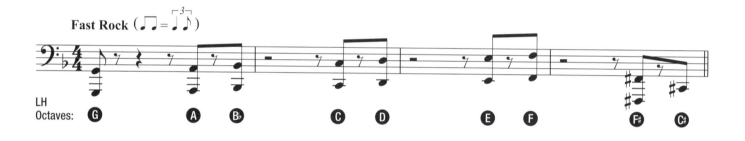

Each measure of the right hand in this pattern is different, but once you learn the chords they feel quite natural and easy to play. Study the keyboard diagram and the music example, and then take your time moving between the chords until you're comfortable playing all four measures.

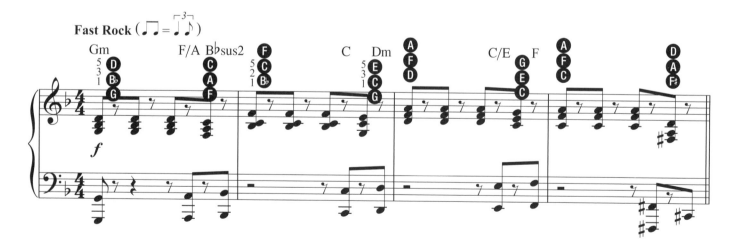

Notice the way the chords are beamed, with an eighth rest in between. Each chord falls squarely on the beat, as you can see by the counting written in. The eighth rests give the chords their snappy feel and create a great sense of energy. The left hand adds to that, bouncing between beats 3 and 4. Dive right in with both hands, playing slowly at first. Try playing along with the audio, slowing the tempo as needed until you're up to speed. These four measures are repeated three more times, though the first verse.

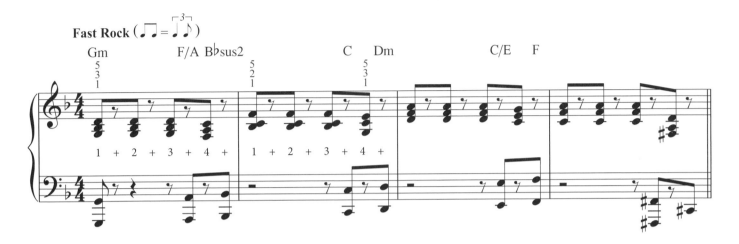

The eight-measure bridge to the chorus will look familiar. It's very similar to the first four measures you just learned. No octaves in the left hand, just the lower notes with a few variations. And, you've learned all the right-hand chords already too.

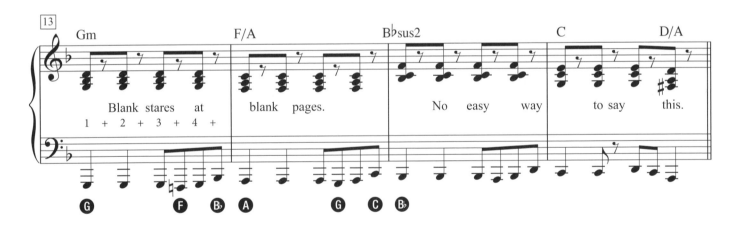

Continue on through the chorus, straight to the end. Use the online audio to help you put everything together. Play along, slowing down the tempo as needed, looping any sections that you find challenging, and sometimes simply listening to the audio for more security with the notes or rhythms.

# LOVE SONG

Words and Music by
SARA BAREILLES

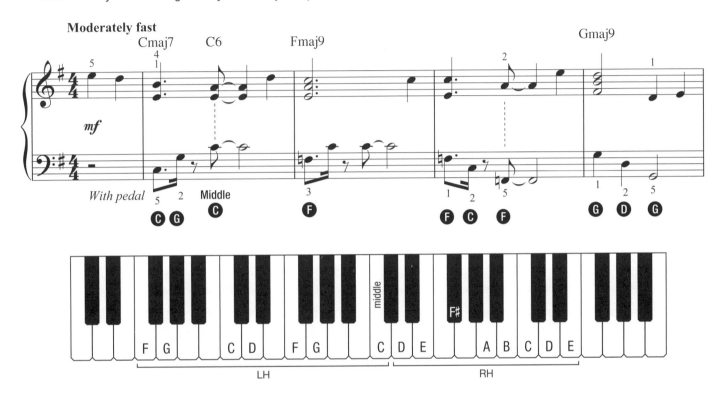

# TEACH YOURSELF LESSON
# ORDINARY PEOPLE

John Legend's jazzy piano ballad has rhythmic drive and colorful harmonies. The left hand moves between octave positions of C, F, and G. Listen to the audio if you need help with the dotted rhythms. Practice along with the left-hand audio to prepare for hands together.

Taking a look at the right hand, notice the syncopation and how it fits with the left hand. When you practice hands together, take it slowly at first and gradually increase your speed.

Moving on with melody and lyrics, you'll notice that the left hand continues the C-F-F-G chord progression; sometimes as it was played in the introduction, and sometimes as intervals of 5th and 7ths. After learning the left hand, practice the right hand alone before you play hands together. Listen to the audio to review any rhythm in the melody you're unsure of.

Girl, I'm in love with you, __ but this ain't the hon - ey - moon. __

We're past the in - fat - u - a - tion phase.

There's a nifty syncopated swing in the melody beginning in measure 12. Notice how the lyrics help you nudge the "and" of beats 2 & 4.

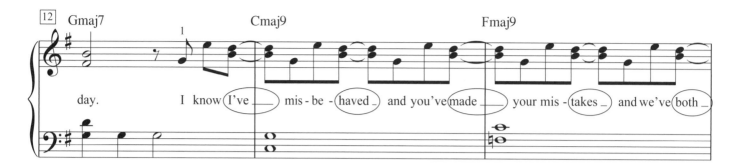

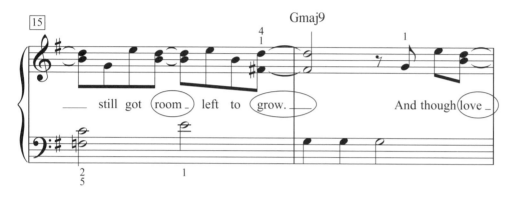

Now, take a look at the right hand at the refrain (measure 21). Although the right hand moves around minimally here, recognizing the intervals in each measure will help you learn the notes more quickly. We've labeled them for you here.

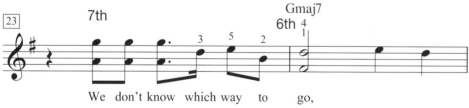

The last section of this song mimics the introduction you've already learned. You're ready to play the entire arrangement.

# ORDINARY PEOPLE

Words and Music by JOHN STEPHENS
and WILL ADAMS

**Moderately fast**

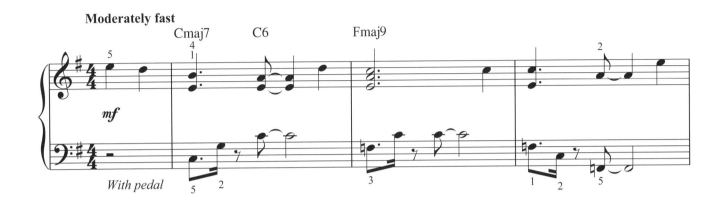

Girl, I'm in love with you, __ but this ain't the hon-ey - moon. __

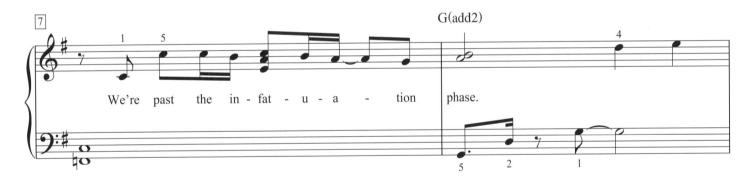

We're past the in-fat-u-a - tion phase.

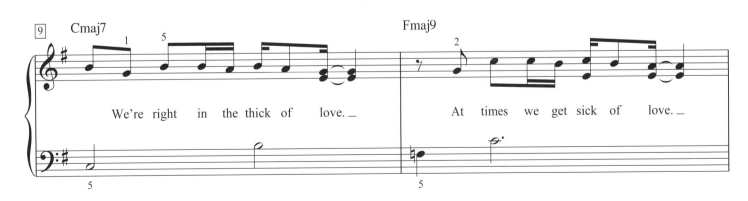

We're right in the thick of love. __ At times we get sick of love. __

# PHILOSOPHY

It's tempting to just jump right into the introduction of this Ben Folds classic, zipping through the right-hand 16th notes, but it takes speed and agility to bring this song to life. We recommend that you play slowly and work with a small group of notes at a time (two beats plus one note). Begin by learning the right hand's first nine notes and practice until this is very comfortable.  Next, start on the note you just ended on and play through the first note of the second measure. Continue in this way through the introduction. Now practice bigger groups of notes (one measure plus one note), gradually increasing the tempo.

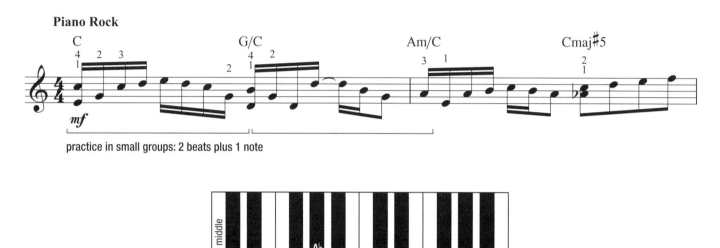

practice in small groups: 2 beats plus 1 note

The rest of the introduction is mostly made up of thirds. We've provided lots of fingering to help you navigate through the measures. Dotted eighths and tied 16th notes give the piece its sparky feel, so if you're unsure of this groove, listen to the audio, or play along with it.

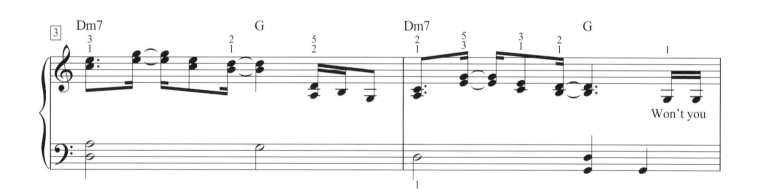

The first lyric motive is played four times with a few slight rhythmic variations. Take some time to get comfortable with the first phrase before moving on. Sing along with the lyrics for some help with the rhythm.

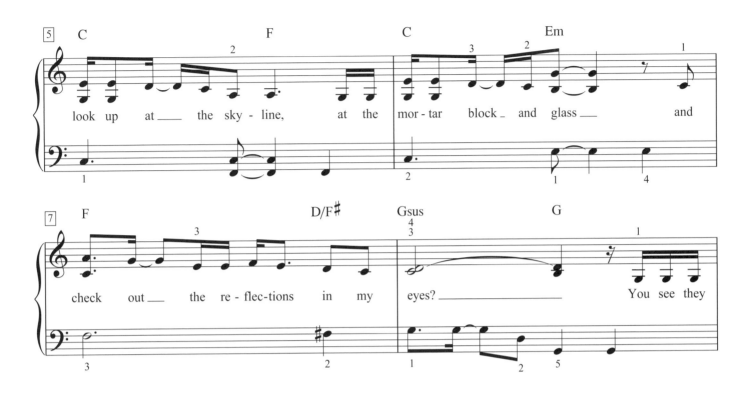

Look ahead through the rest of the song to note similar phrases. In between lyric sections the right-hand part includes some of the fancy finger work you can hear in the original recording. Slow these measures down to work through the fingering until you feel comfortable in spots like these.

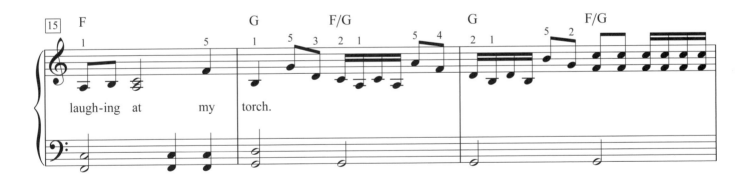

You have advanced to the chorus. The right hand stays pretty close to one position, but the left hand jumps around a bit. Play the left hand alone, or with the right-hand audio part to get a feel for this.

With so much going on in this fun tune, there are many ways to work with the online audio as you learn it. Remember, you can slow the audio down to work on rhythms, and you can isolate and loop tricky sections. Experiment and find what works for you!

# PHILOSOPHY

Words and Music by
BEN FOLDS

# A THOUSAND YEARS

No doubt you're familiar with David Hodges and Christina Perri's beautiful love song from *The Twilight Saga: Breaking Dawn – Part 1* soundtrack. Opening with a haunting piano introduction, it only gets lovelier from there.

The first thing to note is the tempo heading: Moderately, in one. "In one" means that although the time signature indicates 3 beats per measure, you will play with a definite emphasis on beat one, giving the song a feeling of constant forward motion. This is well illustrated right from the beginning of the introduction. The repeated dotted half notes might lead you to believe this song moves slowly, but take a look at the counting we've written in, and listen to the online audio as you follow along. Instead of individual measures of 3, think of four measure phrases, in one.

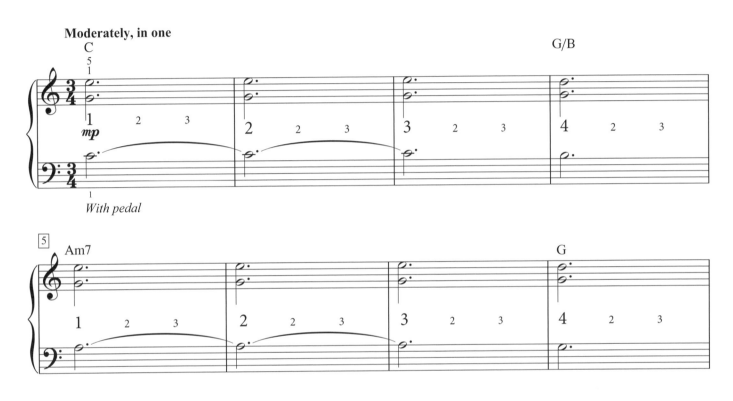

The feeling of one continues at the lyric entrance in measure 17. With left-hand finger 2 on F and thumb on G; and right-hand thumb on middle C, you're anchored for the next section.

As you head into the chorus think about giving the dotted half notes ever-so-slightly more emphasis to propel the harmonies forward.

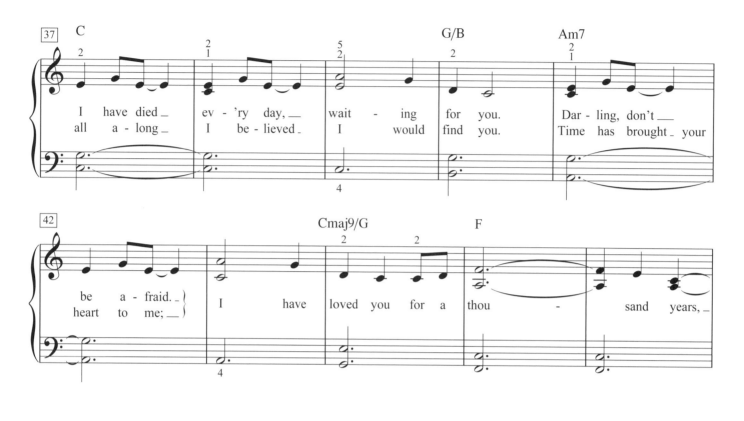

Closing with another beautiful piano solo, bring out the melody notes, listening for the right-hand melody C-B-G played twice over two different harmonies in the left hand, resulting in a poignant but unresolved feeling as you head to the final fermata.

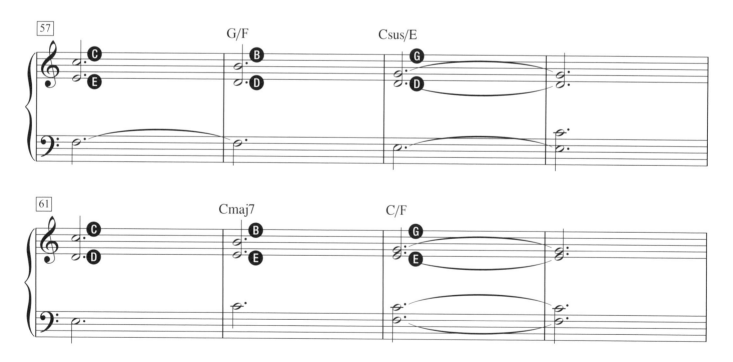

# A THOUSAND YEARS

**from the Summit Entertainment film THE TWILIGHT SAGA: BREAKING DAWN – PART 1**

Words and Music by DAVID HODGES
and CHRISTINA PERRI

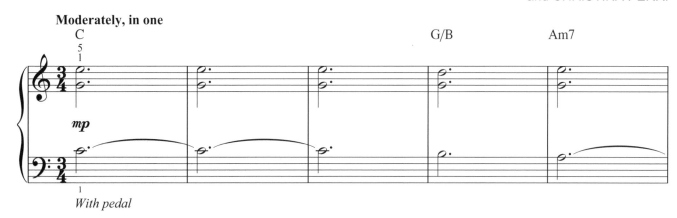

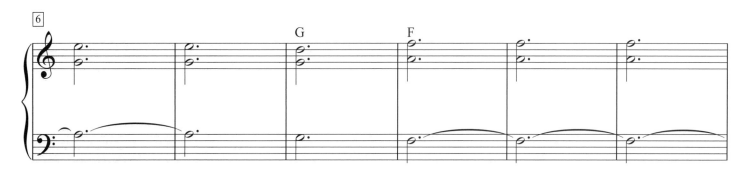

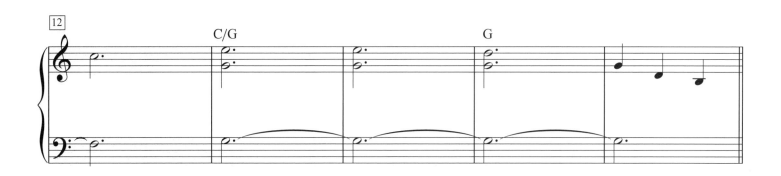

# WHITE HOUSES

This Vanessa Carlton hit relies on the piano to keep the lyrics in motion, particularly in the verse. We've floated the lyrics between the staff so you can sing along. The left hand can relax with repeated notes that start on middle C and move down by step. The right hand looks trickier, but it's very patterned.

Starting with octave Cs for the first four eighth notes, study the right-hand notes we've labeled and the keyboard diagram. You'll notice right away that your right-hand thumb gives you an anchor. While other notes change, you're always playing a C with your thumb. Measures 5-6 are a repeat of measures 3-4.

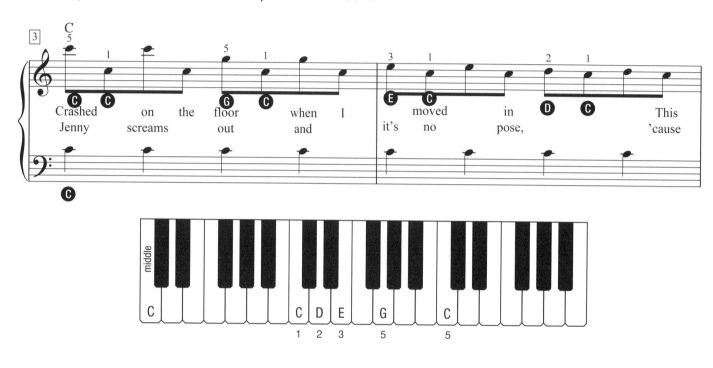

Measures 7-10 are the same as measures 3-6, except your left hand plays B instead of middle C.

The right hand notes change in measures 11-14. Now your right-hand thumb is anchored on A above middle C, and your left-hand thumb plays the A below middle C.

There's one more change to the pattern in measures 15-18. Right-hand thumb and left hand play G.

The second ending brings you to the chorus. Now you've got the melody in the right hand, and a syncopated rhythm to drive you along. The left hand plays the interval of a fifth. It's easy to find the left-hand notes as they correspond to the chord labels above the treble staff. The right hand stays in one place. Lean in a bit to the tied eighth notes, letting the lyrics guide where the emphasis needs to be. Play and sing along with the audio if you need a little help putting this section together.

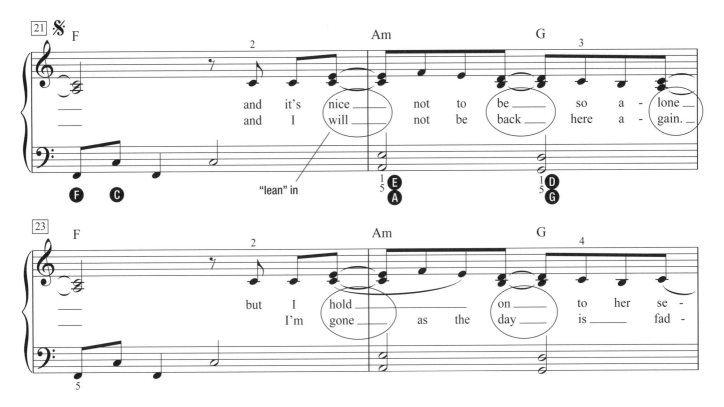

At measure 26 you'll see repeated Cs, signaling a return to material very much like the beginning, and following the sign, you'll be back to the chorus, and the coda, to end the song.

# WHITE HOUSES

Words and Music by VANESSA CARLTON
and STEPHAN JENKINS

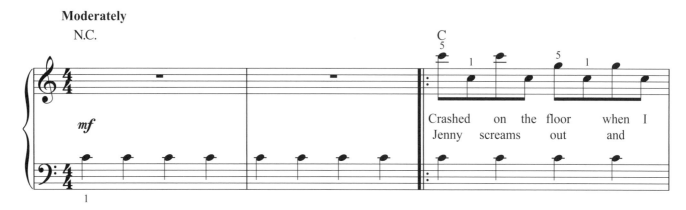

than me.    We gave each other up so    easily.    These

silly little wounds will never mend.    I feel so far from

where I've been. So I go    lie,_____ put my in - jur-ies all \_\_\_ in the dust.\_

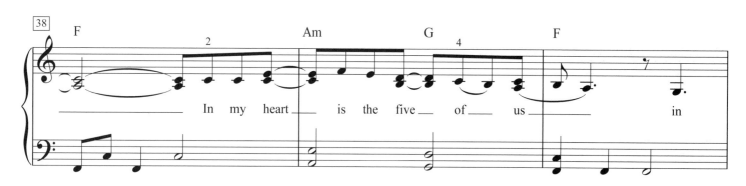

_____ In my heart\_ is the five \_ of \_ us \_\_\_\_\_ in

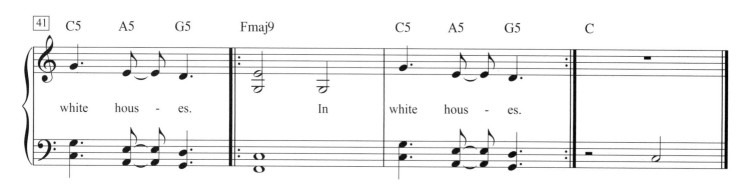

white hous - es.    In white hous - es.